How To Set-Up
Your Personal Brand
For Under $1000

Dan Fleyshman

Table of Contents

Introduction

How To Set-Up Your Personal Brand For Under $1,000

If I asked you to define your personal brand, where would you begin? Most people assume their personal brand is their profession. That's how many people define themselves. Think back to every networking event or mastermind you have ever joined. The first question most of us hear is, "what do you do for work?"

Your personal brand is more than your occupation. Your personal brand is the story of the life you are living and more importantly, telling. Sure, your personal brand should include your profession. But your personal brand is your life resume that follows you forever, even if you decide to start a new venture in a completely new category.

Whether you embrace the possibilities of social media or not, you already have a personal brand. If you picked up this book and are thinking to yourself "I don't have a personal brand," you couldn't be more wrong.

You may not have followers, fans, subscribers and you may not be sharing content online. But you have a personal brand whether you like it or not. You DO have a personal brand; you just might not be telling your story.

The best thing about your personal brand, is that you don't have to be an expert to tell your story. When I first started building my brand, I was known as the youngest founder of a publicly traded company. My first company was an energy drink company and even though that was a long time ago, it's still the opening to my personal brand story.

But my personal brand story is also my charity, social media agency, the companies I invest in and the events we throw. Your personal brand doesn't need to fit in a box. In my opinion, it shouldn't because the world moves too fast. If you are waiting to become an expert in your industry because you don't want to look bad, you might never start.

It might sound like a lot of pressure to start your personal brand because we all want to wait for the right time. The truth is, there will never be a perfect time because the perfect time to start is now. No matter where you are currently in your journey, you deserve to tell your story.

You don't need to know everything to build your personal brand, but you do have to be brave enough to share the authentic truth of your current story. You don't need to be an expert to start. But you do have to start to ever become an expert.

As long as you focus on building your personal brand with integrity, you open yourself to opportunities that otherwise wouldn't have been possible. Your personal brand gives you a platform to test new ideas, launch businesses, create strategic alignments, get paid more for your expertise, speak on platforms and so much more.

Your profession and interests will change as your life changes. But your personal brand will always stay with you. Your personal brand will become a launch pad for everything you will do for the rest of your life, even when you decide to turn your passion into a business.

In 2020, I spotted a trend in sports cards and saw where the future was heading. I loved sports cards as a kid and collected them as a hobby. But now, sports cards were becoming much bigger than a hobby. They were becoming one of the best investments in the marketplace.

Sports cards were starting to trade like athlete stocks. As a player would have more success or increase in popularity, their card price would skyrocket to meet that players demand. There was a nostalgia for people like me who grew up collecting sports cards that were also into investing. It was clear to me that this was going to be a huge opportunity.

At the time, I knew very little about the current marketplace, but there was clearly an interest and an opportunity that I wanted to explore. Many people feel a sense of imposter syndrome when starting to build a personal brand or when that start something new.

But remember, it doesn't have to be perfect and you don't have to be an expert to start. I was far from an expert in the cards industry, but I was willing to share my story and see where it led me. As many of you know, I love poker and I am known to take risks. But I don't gamble without educating myself.

I shared my curiosity and interest in sports cards and decided to meet Gary Vaynerchuk at a sports card convention. One of the great advantages to building a personal brand, is the relationships that you will build with people you meet. Many of those people will be experts in areas that you are not and vice versa.

The plan was to go to a card convention with Gary for a few hours. That couple of hours turned into days and I shared what I was learning about the most coveted sports cards in the world. Lebron James, Kevin Durant, Michael Jordan rookie cards. I was learning everything I could about the industry and what accounted for that players card value.

As I was learning, I would share videos and pictures of what I learned. I was also sharing how I was applying that knowledge. I would share when I bought 100's of Kevin Durant cards and why I bought them. I was combining my passion for sports and knowledge of investing, to build my personal brand in a different category.

I have been building my personal brand for decades, which helps me anytime I launch something new. Over the previous few years, I built my personal brand around my social media agency, my charity Model Citizen and our Mastermind events. Those were just a few of the stories I wanted to tell at that time and those are all a big part of my personal brand still today.

My audience has watched me build all of those businesses, by sharing my story just like this. So, my audience doesn't doubt me when I decide start something completely new. They simply think, "Oh that's just Dan being Dan." They trust me because they have seen me live it over and over again.

Three years ago, I didn't know I would be interested in sports cards. But I did know I would be doing something. That is why it's so important for everyone to think about their own personal brand, even if you don't think your current story is worth telling. Eventually, you will have an idea. If you have a personal brand, it gives you a head start on everyone that doesn't.

Building my personal brand made it simple to tap my friends that were already heavily investing into sports cards. In fact, they were the ones coming to me to tell me about the opportunity because of our relationship. My background in sports, poker and investing created top of mind awareness when sports cards started to trend.

My personal brand allowed me to meet and build relationships with people like Steve Aoki and DJ Skee, who would become my business partners when we launched "Cards & Coffee." It's also the reason we launched with lines outside of the door and had influential people stopping in daily to see the new shop. It didn't hurt that my two partners had very powerful personal brands as well.

Every week, we have new influencers and characters helping grow "Cards & Coffee," because I built my personal brand. All of these years building my social media agency made it simple to call influencers to collaborate in the store.

All of the years sharing about my charity, Model Citizen, made it easy to tie in our contribution with "Cards & Coffee."

Now is the best time to start building your personal brand, even if you don't know what you will use it for. If you are building a personal brand and know what your current goals are, it's likely those will also change in the future as well. Your personal brand is your word, your name and your story. If you focus on building your brand the right way, it will create opportunities for you forever.

Your audience will trust what they see you doing, more than what they hear you say. Building my personal brand has allowed me to build a platform that people trust. When I announce an event, mastermind or investment, my audience wants to know more because they have already seen how I launch new projects.

By sharing the behind the scenes of buying cards, building out a location and creating buzz in the industry, I was creating top of mind awareness. I didn't claim to be an expert in cards right away. I was living my story and documenting my own journey.

If you take away one thing from this book, I hope it's the inspiration to start telling your story from wherever you are right now. This book is designed to help you inspire your own personal brand journey and to start telling others what your personal brand is and will be.

Remember, the goal of a personal brand is to create top of mind awareness so that when people think about buying your product or service, they think about you first. That's how the world works now.

The person who has the most omnipresence, creates the most opportunities. We will talk about the importance of omnipresence throughout the book. Don't allow yourself to rely on your expertise alone. Give people every opportunity to remember your name when they need an expert in your space.

You might be the best real estate agent in North Carolina, but if you are not creating content on Facebook, Instagram, YouTube, TikTok and other platforms, someone else will. If you don't have a personal brand, you are likely missing out on real estate opportunities, along with other opportunities in the future.

For example, what if you decide to stop selling real estate in 5 years? Or let's take it a step further. What if you like real estate and enjoy your job, but also have other side passions that excite you more?

Maybe you make hand-made jewelry with your kids on the weekends. Maybe you love sports cars. Maybe your passion is a charity where you volunteer. Whatever you love to do on the side, you can start to build your personal brand around that.

One day, an influencer decides to repost your handmade jewelry and your Etsy shop explodes with requests. Another day, your car show gets shared on Facebook and you make a connection at a local car dealership. Your video helping your charity goes viral and your local news wants to interview you. Your personal brand is limitless and costs almost nothing.

Think of the opportunities you are missing out on because you are failing to share your personal brand with the world. Think of all of the people that only think of you as just a real estate agent. They don't know about your passion for cars or the work you do for charity. They have no other option because that's what you shared with them on social media.

By not building your personal brand, you are missing out on more than just real estate clients. You are missing out on jewelry clients and more subscribers on your car channels. You are also missing out on opportunities to help your charity.

The best part about building a personal brand? You can build a successful personal brand and tell the world exactly what you do for less than $1000.

The upside of building a personal brand is infinite, because you have no idea what may happen. You might gain new partnerships, investors, retail stores looking for unique local jewelry, a car dealer might want to sponsor your show or somebody like myself might even want to invest in your real estate deals. The upside and opportunities are limitless, but they can't exist without you building your personal brand.

The downside of building a personal brand? Nothing. The time and money commitments are minimal, and the upside is limitless. If you know my story, you know by now about my background in gambling. By building a personal brand, my risk is nothing and the upside is infinite.

Imagine that you go to Las Vegas, and they tell you that you can win millions of dollars playing blackjack. Then they tell you that you won't risking anything but your time sitting at the table. I would take the opportunity every time, and I hope you would do the same.

Let's take this a step further and suppose you say "I don't have any hobbies or side hustles I want to share with the world. I only love real estate and work 80 hours per week."

Even if your personal brand centers around real estate, you still deserve to build your personal brand.

There are plenty of professionals building powerful personal brands around their profession. If that is the story you want to tell, then tell it. Make sure your personal brand showcases what separates you from your competition.

Imagine someone tells one of your friends that they are in the market for a home. That friend knows a few people that do real estate and you are one of them. The problem for you is their other friend has built a strong personal brand. They post videos every day on Facebook and share pictures of recently sold homes on Instagram. They also post daily real estate tips on LinkedIn and have a YouTube channel teaching people how to buy their dream home.

You may have better real estate credentials, but who do you think they will think about first?

When you develop your personal brand, you are creating top of mind awareness with every person you meet. Whether you like it or not, every person you interact with thinks of you as your personal brand.

In fact, even people you don't know or people that are exposed to you for the first time, whether on social media or in person, think about you as your personal brand. In each of those circumstances, you must be able to tell your story.

Whether they think about you once, sometimes or always, it should be told efficiently and effectively because you might not get a second chance.

First impressions are everything. If you can't quickly share the story of your personal brand, they will draw conclusions on their own. You don't want someone else telling your story, even to themselves. Once somebody has made up their mind, it can be difficult to change that narrative.

How To Use This Book

This book was designed to be a practical guide to help you start and launch your personal brand. It was written to be consumed in order and there are workshop checklists throughout the chapters to keep you on track towards building your personal brand.

The strategies in this book are the same strategies I have used to build my own personal brand. The same strategies I use to launch all of my ventures to this very day. Remember, your personal brand story will change, but it will always be yours.

While writing this book, "Cards & Coffee" has turned into a franchise business with multiple-locations and growing. I created a new layer for my personal brand and my story.

Before we dive into the rest of the book, here is how I share the structure of my own personal brand, anytime someone asks who I am and what I do.

"I was the youngest founder of a publicly-traded company in history at the age of 23. I didn't sleep for the next 5 years, and I got our products into 55,000 retail stores. Then, I started an online poker site and built it to be the 3rd largest poker brand in the world.

I became an angel investor in 36 companies. I started a social media agency where we spend over $60 million with influencers. Finally, my main passion is my charity, Model Citizen Fund. We create backpacks for the homeless with 150 emergency supplies inside."

That may sound like a lot, but don't get overwhelmed. This story was developed through years of hard work and you will develop the layers of your own story. If you don't currently have a story, don't let that stop you. I am going to show you exactly how to create your story.

I will also show you how to create the content, connections and resources to share your story with the world. There are layers in my story that share exactly what I have done, what I am doing now and my level of contribution back to the world. No matter who I meet, they will understand how we can collaborate or work together.

Chapter 1:

Crafting Your Story

Every word in my personal brand story is intentional because I may only get 30 seconds to share it. Start thinking of your personal brand like this as well, by defining your own story. The first sentence should grab your audience's attention. Think of this as your headline that will entice somebody to read more.

"Youngest Founder of a publicly-traded company in history"

That sentence grabs the audience's attention because nobody else had accomplished what I had at that age. That may have been 15 years ago, but it still serves as a headline that grabs the audience's attention right away. It is also a line that people can remember and easily share if someone else asks them "who was the speaker you saw."

At the very least, they will remember I was the youngest founder of a publicly-traded company in history. They can share that piece of information, which may encourage that next person to look up who I am. Many people still explain my personal brand with that one sentence.

The rest of my personal brand story is intentional as well. For example, when I say I didn't sleep for 5 years, I then explain why. It's important that people understand the level of sacrifice it took to get where I am today. Every day people are coming across me that don't know my story, whether in real life or on social media. My past successes establish credibility with someone seeing me for the first time.

I then share my current business ventures as an angel investor, along with my social media agency. If someone wants to work with me, they know exactly what I do, and it allows us to move the conversation to the next level.

Finally, I save my main passion for last because I want it to be the emotional connection they remember the most. Many of the people I meet have already found success in their businesses. Now they want to find more ways to contribute to society. If someone wants to donate time, money or energy to my charity, I want to make sure they know exactly what we do and how we do it.

This elevator pitch might seem simple, but you would be surprised how many people fail to effectively explain who they are and what they do. My goal is to inspire people to quickly take action and create momentum after reading this book. If you already have a story and a business, start by writing out your own personal brand story. Refine it so that you can share your full story next time somebody asks, "what do you do?"

Chapter 2:

Your Digital Real Estate

Once you develop your personal brand story, start to lock down your social media handles on each platform. Also, make sure your brand story is the same on each platform. People often make the mistake of being one person on Instagram and a different person on LinkedIn.

It's easy to lose trust with somebody just meeting you if they see two completely different people on different platforms. By locking in your digital real estate and building out your bio, you are creating momentum to keep going.

After you establish your social media handles, build out a website for your personal brand. Building a website isn't as expensive or complicated as it used to be, but it is essential for your personal brand.

Social media is a great place to tell your story in pieces, but your brand needs a home that tells your full story. Your website will showcase what you do, past successes, your social proof and a contact form to reach out to you.

You can find an entry-level developer on a site like Upwork/Fiverr or collaborate with someone you know. If that isn't an option, create your own using a site builder like WIX.

People will get to know you on social media but will want to know the depth of your story if they intend to work with you. Make sure to purchase a domain name that matches your name or your personal brand name.

While you are building out your own digital real estate, don't forget about your family members and kids. If your daughter is three years old, you probably are not thinking about her building an Instagram account. However, you may want to go ahead and reserve their website URL and social media names.

Why? Let's say you don't reserve their name and someone else does. What if that person ends up being an axe murderer?

Now, every time someone Googles her name, which they will, your daughter is labeled alongside an axe murderer simply because you didn't claim her digital real estate.

Start to think about the people you care about most and claim their social media handles. It costs nothing but could save them from pain in the future. This might be an extreme example, but you get the point. Claim your future kids brand names so that an axe murderer doesn't.

Finally, get a Linktree to make every platform easy to find and a Calendly account to schedule calls. Instead of sending out 8 links to everyone you meet, Linktree will host your links in one place. Think of Linktree as a mini-website where people can find your social media handles. It also showcases your email and your website all in one place. Once they find your social accounts and visit your website, they can come back to your Linktree and book a call.

Workshop: Your Digital Real Estate

1. Establish your personal brand story
2. Lock in your social media handles
3. Make the bio and photo the same on all platforms
4. Buy a URL for your website
5. Create a blog or personal website
6. Create a Calendly scheduling account
7. Get a Linktree for easy accessibility

Build Out Your Website

Building out your website and one-page PDF is essential for growing your personal brand. Now that you have developed your personal brand story and locked your social media handles, it's time to begin establishing your web presence and expanding on your story.

What else have you done? What do you currently do? Where can people learn more about you? Where have they seen you? Press? Podcasts?

Without meeting someone, the goal of your one-page website is to gain trust and clarity on what you do. You will also establish credibility and create authority in your industry. Eventually, this website and one page will be your resource to pitch your story.

In a later chapter, I will share how to use your website to pitch podcasts, press outlets, speaking events and other platforms. These platforms are all essential for building your personal brand.

Workshop: Your One-Page Website

1. Name & personal brand story
2. Social media links
3. Photos of yourself
4. Work/services you offer
5. Podcasts you have appeared on
6. Press you have received
7. Media appearances/T.V.
8. Testimonials
9. Questions they should ask you
10. Charities/Contributions
11. Contact page to reach out

Think of this as your modern-day resume and answer to the question "Why me?" Podcasts, press outlets, events, radio, newspapers and television networks receive hundreds, if not thousands of pitches each month. It's your job to break through that noise with a compelling story and social proof.

Your goal is to show them why your story is worth telling. Why should they interview you? What makes your story special? Why would an audience listen to your story and expertise for 45 minutes?

Chapter 3:

Developing Your Personal Brand Story

I often hear the question, "Dan, what if I don't have a resume or compelling story like you do?"

Everyone has to start somewhere, including me. Before I had the story and resume I do now, I was the guy hustling every day to build my drink company. I wasn't investing in other businesses and I didn't have a digital marketing agency.

Instead, I was spending every minute working and building my business. For most of you, that is the story you can tell. Document your journey of building your business and not only the wins. Share your authentic story with the world as you are building your business.

Maybe one day your company lands a new retail client and you tell the story of that excitement. Then the next week your inventory gets lost in transit and causes chaos for your business.

In my personal brand story, I share that I didn't sleep for five years. People want to see the difficult times you go through, not only the success. Perfect businesses and perfect lives don't exist. When you share your vulnerabilities with the world, you create a deeper, more relatable connection with your audience. The easiest way to create content is to document what you are doing every day.

If you don't currently have a business or side hustle to share with the world, then start by throwing an event. Brainstorm what your niche needs or throw a charity event that will attract people into your network. Charity events create goodwill for a good cause. Charity events become part of your personal story, generate content and allow you to network with local authorities in your city.

If your goal is to get press, news or land podcast appearances, you must create awareness around who you are. You also need a compelling story to tell. The people you are pitching receive hundreds of story pitches every week. It's your job to get their attention.

If your personal story isn't compelling enough, and you don't have a brand, then I recommend throwing a charity event. You will be supporting a cause you care about in your community and may get the attention of local press outlets. Even if that doesn't happen, you are starting to build the story of your personal brand.

Let's take Khloe Kares for example. When she was 8 years old, Khloe started her non-profit organization with her mom. She throws charity events, serves her local community, does global outreach and even wrote a few children's books. She decided she wanted to make an impact on the world and started her own charity. It didn't cost a lot of money, it just required effort, will and perseverance to get Khloe Kares off the ground.

Unknowingly, she was making a huge impact on the community and eventually I heard what she was doing. I was so inspired that we decided to throw an event together with my charity, Model Citizen. Our goal was to raise money and awareness for three local organizations in the Los Angeles area. The event was a huge success and Khloe's name continues to grow because she got started on her own.

Khloe is 13 years old and already has more press than most people I know. Last year, she was even featured on the Today Show for her charity work in LA and Chicago.

If you are building a personal brand, your story and impact on the world will become your personal brand. You can do that through charity, business or other creative contributions. It must be authentic and interesting if your goal is to build an omnipresent personal brand.

Adding a layer to your personal brand

It's essential to add a layer of depth for your personal brand. You want to let people know how they can work with you or contribute to your charity, when building your brand.

For example, you can start your own podcast and create your own brand. But, what's next? If people love your podcast, they will want to find out what else you do and how they can work with you.

Let's take Casey Adams for example. Casey Adams started his podcast "Rise Of The Young" when he was 17 years old. He was excited and eager to build his personal brand, but he didn't know what it would become. I jumped on his podcast and started introducing him to other guests. Casey made the smart move by adding an extra layer to his brand. Instead of just interviewing authorities, Casey went and started throwing live events and doing business outside of his podcast. Now, instead of just meeting influential people, he has something to say when someone asks, "what do you do?"

If you are in Casey's position, wondering what layer you should add, consider throwing your first event in your community. If you are already a real estate agent, then throw a local real estate event. If you have no idea what you want to do or don't currently have a business, then align with your favorite charity and throw a local charity event. These events don't have to be huge and don't need much money to start.

Chapter 4:

Planning Your First Event

If you are throwing your first event, first decide whether it will be an industry event or charity event. When I say industry event, I mean real estate, cooking, stock trading, etc. Decide on your niche, theme and goals for your event. Once you understand that, you can focus on those types of guests.

Next, figure out the capacity for your event. For your first event, don't overwhelm yourself. Try to keep the event around 50 to 100 people. If your ambition is to throw 1000 person events right away, those can get very expensive and are not necessary. If you invite 50-100 of the right people, you will have the same impact at far less cost, especially when you land a few sponsors for the event.

Once you know how many people you expect to invite, then you can start looking for a venue and date for the event. Personally, I throw most of my events on Monday through Thursday.

If it is a charity event, you can do Sunday during the day time. I rarely do Friday/Saturday because there's far more competition.

What do I mean by competition?

Competition for affordable venue space and also your guests' schedules.

Fridays and Saturdays are the most sought-after days for event venues. Attendees are also the most likely to be busy on weekends with trips, sports, activities, etc. Vendors are more in demand on weekends as well.

Choosing a weekend will be more costly and more difficult to lock in vendors for your event. On a Tuesday, your vendors and venue are far more likely to accommodate your needs because they're less busy.

If you are throwing your first event, you want the least resistance possible for your venue, vendors and guests. Stick to Monday-Thursday if at all possible. When you start looking for an event venue, you want your venue to be cool.

What do I mean by cool?

If I sent you an invite saying, "meet me at the Westin Inn ballroom," you probably wouldn't be very excited. But, if I said, "meet me at a mansion in Hollywood Hills," you are more likely to show up.

If you go the traditional venue route, they will probably charge you because that's how they do business. It would be difficult to land a corporate hotel ballroom for free. However, you might have a friend that has a mansion and wants to be part of the charity event.

A referral or friend with a mansion is always my first choice if possible. People like hosting other affluent people at their homes. It allows them to connect with people and their cost is nothing because they own the home. It's also a fantastic way to ensure the event converts because people will be more likely to come.

Wherever the venue is, you will need to convince the host on why they should allow you to host an event there. You can pitch them on the fact that you're bringing 100 people in the real estate, crypto, or stock market space. Whatever your niche is, they will likely be interested.

If a mansion or location isn't easily accessible, don't let that keep you from throwing your event. Start searching for a warehouse, art gallery, museum, family center or other unique locations in your town. You might need to get creative with your approach. Check the local photographers and videographers. Look on their social media accounts and see where they film or where they photograph.

After that, search for those locations on Google. You're going to find unique places in your area. Search different keyword terms like "cool venue Alabama" or "unique warehouse Alabama." Additionally, you can also start pre-promoting the event in the process by asking your social media following. "what's a cool venue to throw my charity event?"

You are organically starting to promote your event to your following. If you pick the location they recommended, they are more likely to attend because they had a say in the planning process.

The more unique the location is, the more likely you are to convert people. On top of that, the unique location will equal better content during the event. If you need to book a restaurant or hotel, do it.

If all else fails, use a site like Peerspace. Venues will cost a few hundred dollars and you will know exactly what you are getting into.

Planning & Promoting the Event

Now that you have locked down your venue, it's time to plan and promote the event. When you start to tease the location and tell people that you are throwing an event, curiosity will set in.

People will naturally start asking for more information about the event. Don't tell them what it is quite yet. Instead, just say your charity event, real estate event or your cars event. Keep the curiosity and intrigue high.

They will be more excited once you finally announce the event. At this point you will start getting interest from guests and sponsors. People may start asking how to attend and how to buy tickets.

For your first event, you don't need to sell tickets and I wouldn't recommend it. This event is for networking, contribution and building your brand.

But on the ticket front, keep this in mind. You can make a ticket price that's $20, $50, $100 or more, even if you don't sell them. The reason for that is that you create an implied value when you comp people the ticket.

Elevator Nights has a $100 ticket and a $500 ticket. I don't even have a checkout page, you couldn't buy a ticket if you wanted to, and I've had that for 38+ events.

So when I give somebody two $500 tickets, I just gave them $1000. If I give somebody four $100 tickets, I gave them $400, even though there's literally no way you could buy those tickets.

Emotionally, this is important when it comes to the invites and setting ticket prices. It will also help with conversion because of the perceived value of the $100 ticket. People are more likely to attend because of the $100 value and you will create a lot of personal equity with that person.

People don't typically value free. So, if you start giving away tickets for free, then your event becomes an option instead of a priority. However, if they think they just got a $100 ticket, they are far more likely to show up to the event.

Next, it's time to book your speakers and headliners for the event. If you are throwing your first event, it's likely that your name won't get people excited about coming. You will be the host and person responsible for the event, but you want to land a few headline names to attract people to attend.

Let's say you start cold calling or driving to locations to invite people. Let's say you're doing a car-related event. You are obsessed with cars and want to throw an event based on cars. You just landed a new job at the local exotic car dealership and cars are your life.

Your goal is to try to get Manny Khoshbin to be your speaker. Manny has $30 million in cars in his garage and you know his name would attract everyone in the area that loves cars.

You should reach out to Manny, but you should also reach out to Ben Baller and 20 other people. Reach out to anyone that has authority in your industry that lives within a one-hour radius. Think of personal brands that seem interested in speaking and personal branding.

You will find out very quickly that these guys will want to know who else is speaking at the event. You will want to create implied value for your event based on other speakers and attendees. Nobody wants to be the first speaker to commit.

However, if you can land one firm commitment, you can share their names with every other potential speaker and attendee. If you land people like Manny Khosbin and Ben Baller, your event will snowball into a huge success.

Next thing you know, the entire dealership is full of supercars which creates an exciting and content-rich setting for your event.

This is why you want to move as fast as possible. You want to invite everyone within a few hours of asking a Manny Khosbin. He might be your top priority, but you may end up with two, three or ten people just because you got that first yes.

Manny Khosbin may be the first person to respond, asking "who are the other speakers in attendance?" You may not have anyone else lined up yet, but 30 minutes later, Ben Baller is available and says he would love to attend. Now, you can respond to Manny and you will start gaining real momentum for your event.

Once you get commitments from speakers, then you want to start contacting sponsors. Now that you have headline speakers, sponsors are far more likely to say yes. Instead of an unknown event, there is value and exposure by tying their brand to these speakers. The sponsors will also be excited about the content and exposure they will gain from the event.

Most of the time, you will have a higher success rate than you think. People enjoy going to events. They especially enjoy charity events where they can socialize with affluent colleagues. Many of them also want to make an impact on their community.

Some may want to come for their own ego or personal brand. Some may just want to check a box and feel like they are doing good in the community. Some will want to donate to the cause and create a deep connection with your charity.

Don't worry if your first event isn't huge, you have to start somewhere. Our first Model Citizen event had 6 volunteers, and now we average over 150 volunteers. Today, we fill up entire warehouses of donations for charity and people love being part of these events.

You might be pleasantly surprised how fast word of mouth spreads when you start inviting people to your event.

Our first Elevator Night was upstairs at a retail store. I didn't know what to expect and the room could only hold 60 people. Over 150 people showed up because word spread so quickly. Often times, your event becomes bigger than you because people want to be associated with your event.

People want to have access and association with the event, so they will end up reaching out to their network on your behalf.

In reality, they are reaching out on their behalf, but before you know it, word spreads and you end up with far more attendees than you had planned for. That first event has now led to 38 Elevator Nights.

Throwing these industry-related or charity events compels guests to think about you. They will remember this event six months from now, a year from now, two years from now. Those memories will relate back to you and that's how you as the host, build a memorable personal brand.

Workshop: Planning Your Event

What is your niche or charity you want to be known for?

Who is your ideal speaker? Who is your ideal attendee?

What location do you want to land for your event?

Who is your ideal sponsor for the event?

How will you invite and attract attendees?

Chapter 5:

Setting Up Your First Event

Before you launch your event, you will want to promote the event and let everyone know the details. You should create a landing page, social banners and decide how many people you want to attend.

Remember, for your first event, don't bite off more than you can handle. I know you are excited to launch your brand and event to the world. But, if the event is too large, it may get expensive and won't allow you to network with the right people.

You might be tempted to invite every person you know, but don't. I would rather you have 44 people, instead of 68 with the other 24 being cousins, uncles and friends. Remember, this is not a happy hour. This is your opportunity to network and build quality relationships with people in your niche.

You want your run of show to be three hours because anything longer will burn people out. The mistake most people make, is they assume more time means more networking. In reality, if your event extends to 4-6 hours, you risk people leaving early or showing up late because of the broad time frame.

If you notice, Elevator Nights have always been the same time, 7:00 PM to 10:00 PM and I run it like a machine. The event starts with networking at 7 o clock, and the first speaker is on stage by 7:30. At 9:59, I'm saying goodbye and we're done.

Sure, people will linger, but at that point, it's their choice to stay longer. I leave the first half-hour for networking, have a break at 8:45 and wrap up by 9:59. You want to be firm with these times because as you will see, it's easy to get carried away once the event begins.

You can use that similar model, or something similar, to cater to your own event. Whether it's charity poker, a 5K, a charity walk, drop-offs or donations, 3 hours is the magic window I have discovered that works for almost everyone.

Even Hollywood understands that magic 3-hour window. When you go to the movies, two hours is a sweet spot, and if it's great, three hours will work, but anything beyond that begins to drain your audience.

The next decision you will need to make is finding a photographer and videographer. Remember, you are running the event for charity or to serve your niche. But you are also running it to create content for your website and personal brand.

Find a creative that will capture all of the moments from the event. If you do this the right way, you will capture enough content to use for the next year. Ask around or search for talent on social media.

There is a chance they may want to be paid. If you have curated a great speaker lineup and audience, they may do it for free. Creators are often open to collaboration under the right terms. They may film your event in exchange for meeting your headline speakers.

Make sure that when you do land on a photographer, they know your goals for capturing content. Get photos and videos of you in action, on stage, hosting and greeting people. Make sure to stop and take photos with the speakers and any key players that attend the event.

For example, If the local mayor to stops by your charity event or if the CEO of Caldwell Banker comes by your real estate event. You want to make sure to get those photos and videos together with that person.

You can also use those images and videos to follow up with any of those key players you want to continue building a relationship with. There is no better way to get a response than to send a text or message with a high-quality photo or edited video from your event.

Remember, you put in a lot of hard work to get these people together. Make sure you give yourself every opportunity to build on those relationships. Your goal is to create a memorable impression with everyone in attendance.

Once you throw that first event, your second event is going to be infinitely better and easier because now you've gone through the process. Your social proof will help you promote future events with the images and videos. Now when you invite people, it becomes a no brainer because they see you have already done it before.

From a cost production side, you don't need to be fancy and it doesn't need to be extravagant. The reason I recommend 50-100 people is because you want to be in control of the event. If there are key players at your event, take the opportunity to introduce them to each other. Become a bridge for these relationships.

People have built multi-million-dollar careers being great people connectors. For that reason, don't just invite everyone to your event. Throw your event with intention and invite the key players in the real estate industry (or niche). Invite people that live within an hour of your event location.

It might be tempting to do this the easy way, by just blasting out a post and telling friends to tell friends. Again, this isn't a happy hour. If you set your intentions to network and curate the right audience, it will require some hard work on your part. But it will all be worth it.

Spend time on the phones, DM's, emails, texts and do whatever is necessary to convince the right people to come. Your first event will be the most difficult, but if you do the hard work upfront, your future events will be much easier.

While you're doing this, it will be easy to get stuck in your head. Anytime you are doing something new, you will feel imposter syndrome take over.

Remember, this is your time to put yourself on a pedestal and edify yourself. This is your event and YOU are the host. You deserve to feel that confidence because of how hard you have worked to put the event together.

When I throw events, I usually block off a full day where I sit and text hundreds of people. I make my social media posts too, but I also use what I call, hand to hand combat. If I hand text them or call them personally, the conversion rate of them showing up is through the roof.

If I just post about it on social media, a lot of people will show up. But, if I want my main characters to come, I invite them directly to make sure they will attend.

Creating Your Invite Page

Your social media banners are important because they are easily shareable. You also want to solidify the event by creating a landing page with a shareable invite link. If this is your first event use events.com because they host everything you will need in one place. It's like utilizing twelve different apps all in one place.

The event landing page needs to have extreme clarity, and this isn't the place to get too "busy" or overly creative. Don't get fancy with calligraphy text or special graphics. You want this to be decisive and direct by answering the key questions about your event.

Include the point of the event, the name, any key speakers/guests and any key details about the event. For example, is the event for charity? Should they bring anything? Is it a black-tie event? You don't want your guests to feel uncomfortable because they didn't dress up after a casual day at the office.

Chapter 6:

Making Your Event A Success

On the days leading up to the event, you are going to start feeling all kinds of emotions. Excitement, nervousness and everything that comes with the unknown. You will also feel tempted to project an over-confidence to everyone coming to the event. My best advice is to under-promise and over-deliver.

What do I mean by that?

Don't say that 300 people are coming if you only expect 100 people to show up because then you will feel like you failed.

Instead, if you say 50 people are coming, and 100 people show up, the event is a huge success. The same idea goes for your charity events. It might be exciting to say you are going to raise $50,000 for charity, but if you only raise $17,000, it will feel like you failed.

If your goal was $10,000, it will feel like a monumental success. Don't limit your idea of success. But for your first event, you want to set the expectations to under-promise and over-deliver.

On the day of the event, make sure you arrive at the venue early to set up shop. Make sure you have your vendors do the same. If your event starts at 2:00, don't show up at 1:45 and expect everything to be set up.

Even if the venue assures you they have it handled. You will find that something is almost guaranteed to not go as planned. A vendor will show up late, the WIFI will be out, the chairs didn't show up or something along those lines.

Remember, you are committing to be solution-oriented and make this event a success. When something goes wrong, don't sit and cry about it. If the food truck is late because he broke down on the highway, pull up your Postmates app, order food or call a local vendor to step in. Don't spotlight the problems for everyone to see, especially not your speakers or guests.

There will always be things that go wrong when throwing events. You are building your personal brand, so you don't want to talk about the errors or drama going on in the background. Your guests don't need to hear that the vendors and food people are arguing with each other. Who cares? That's not for anybody to know besides you.

Have extreme clarity with your staff & schedule

Remember I mentioned earlier that things will get chaotic on event day? For that reason, you must have extreme clarity with your staff and a strict schedule for your event. If a speaker is supposed to hit the stage at 8:30, make sure you tell them 8 o clock or 7:30.

Always invite them an hour prior to when you actually need them because again, stuff happens. People are late, they get stuck in traffic, they start doing their hair for too long and the list goes on. Elevator Nights are typically in Los Angeles, so I always plan for delays and late arrivals.

Your schedule is the lifeblood of your event, which is why the hour cushion is so important. When I run events, I have a hard schedule planned down to the minute. I know exactly what time each speaker is going on stage and who is speaking when. That is just for me to know though, because again, things could change, and nobody will know but me.

For that reason, I don't leverage all of my guests in case somebody can't make it at the last minute. I usually only leverage one or two guests and keep the rest a surprise.

When I throw our Mastermind events, it's a $100,000 event per person. They don't know who is speaking until they walk on stage. At our last event, we had 14 speakers and they didn't know a single one ahead of time.

My partner didn't know Kris Jenner was speaking because I didn't tell him. If she wasn't going to show, then nobody would know the difference. However, if she was the headline speaker and couldn't make it, people may be disappointed. Keep that in mind when you host your events and remember to under-promise, over-deliver.

The run of show is so important for your event and you should have a hard flow of time, even if nobody else knows what that is. Make sure you are blunt with your speakers about their time frame as well. Speakers are known to be long-winded and they will often feel tempted to drag on past their time.

You can't let that happen because it impacts the next speaker and the entire flow of your event. Nothing feels worse than reaching the end of your event time with two speakers left to speak. Those speakers probably won't be very excited to come back and speak at your next event.

During the event, always remember, you are the host and you are in control. This will allow you to make sure you don't fall behind with your schedule. Don't hire a host, YOU are the host. You are building your personal brand. Make sure you are the one introducing them on stage and seeing them off after speaking. This allows you to stay in control, while also branding yourself as the leader of the event.

Being the host of the event doesn't mean that you make the experience all about you. In fact, it means the opposite. Make sure that you make the event about everyone else. You are just the person in control of making that experience possible. Check on everybody in the room. Make sure people feel included. Make introductions where necessary and ask your guests if you can get them anything. Curate the experience so that it is memorable for everyone in attendance.

Make sure to get people together in photos and direct your photographer beforehand. You want people taking pictures together as much as possible. If you have key players in attendance, get them together for a photo and create those relationships.

People will always remember who introduced them to each other. Also, those photos become a great excuse to follow up the next day when you thank them for attending.

When you follow up with those photos, guess what happens? They again remember the experience they had the night before. They will likely post the photos and either tag you, talk about you or think about you. It's usually all three, which is exactly what you hoped for when you set out to throw your live event.

Remember, this doesn't mean to just take photos of the two of you together. Take photos of them with friends, their spouse, other speakers and so on. If you send these photos out to the key players in attendance, they will likely both tag you. Better yet, they will think about you long after the event is over.

It's also essential to get one great piece of signage. If possible, a branded step and repeat wall is the best way to go. Why? Because every photo will have your brand logo, along with the sponsors and your charity in the background.

Signage is usually one of your only costs of the event besides food and beverages. It's the best investment you can make for your event and personal brand. That becomes your red-carpet entryway for everyone in attendance. Every photo will have your logos in the background and be a branded memory of your event.

Chapter 7:

Creating & Distributing Your Content

If you're starting to build your personal brand, it's important to understand the term omnipresence. If people don't know what you do, they can't do business with you. Additionally, if they don't think of you immediately when they think about your niche, then you have more work to do.

The only way to create omnipresence for your personal brand is to be visible everywhere. We are living through the age of social media. While television, billboards and radio are still viable platforms, they cost a lot of money. They also cast a broad net with people that may or may not care about what you have to say.

Social media allows you to find your niche and create content that serves that niche. The best part is that it's

FREE. You can literally reach millions of people interested in your niche and it costs nothing.

If you have the drive to build a personal brand, and a willingness to create content, then no goal is too big. There are TikTok stars that made millions of dollars last year. They did it by creating funny videos or dancing because that's what they love to do.

At this point, you likely have a library of pictures and videos that you can use for months. On top of that, you will have created a ton of confidence from your first successful event. You might even be inspired to keep creating new content. The event is a great way to build your initial following and exposure. Now it's time to expand and grow your personal brand.

What is Omnipresence?

Omnipresence is when you are everywhere all of the time. No matter where people search, they see your content and your brand. Anytime somebody thinks of your niche, they think about you. In real life, that's impossible, but social media has allowed access to make the impossible a reality.

If your goal is omnipresence, that means you should be publishing content to every major platform. That means

Twitter, Facebook, Instagram, YouTube, LinkedIn, TikTok, and Snapchat. That also includes podcasting, Clubhouse, blogs, press, and everywhere your audience consumes content.

If that sounds like a lot of work, it can be, but it doesn't have to be. Instead of getting overwhelmed, think about creating something valuable. A video aimed to help your audience, preferably. Then repurpose your content on every platform.

What do I mean to repurpose?

If I create a video, I will publish it on Instagram first. I will also publish that video on Facebook, LinkedIn, Twitter, Snapchat and maybe TikTok as well, depending on the video. Now, instead of creating six different videos, I only made one. But I published it to six places to give that video the best opportunity to be seen by as many people as possible.

That is how you repurpose content, with the eventual goal to become omnipresent. You become omnipresent by building a following on those different channels.

Don't be a repurposing robot. If people don't see you using each platform natively, they won't engage with you and they won't follow you for long. Instead, repurpose content as the top of your funnel strategy. Then use each platform natively as your time allows.

Natively means "as it was intended to." Meaning, if every Twitter post is a repost link from Instagram, people are not likely to engage with you. Repurpose everywhere you can, but make sure to also curate content for each platform.

Once you test each platform, you will also start to see where your content is performing the best. Performance will be a great indicator of where you should spend your time and energy.

For example, if you are an aspiring sportswriter looking to have your articles noticed, Twitter is probably the platform for you.

If you are a fashion blogger, looking to share your style tips and pictures of your clothes, Instagram is the best place.

Once you know your niche and start publishing content, your engagement will tell you which platforms are the best use of your energy.

Here is a breakdown of every platform and which content performs best on each of those platforms.

Chapter 8:

The Platforms

Twitter

If newspapers are dying, it's because people are getting their news somewhere else. For many people, they are getting news from Twitter, the social watercooler of our time.

Twitter is where people go to see what's going on in the world. Whether that's politics, sports, video games, current events, weather or anything current. That's Twitter, the fast and furious place of current where people don't spend long periods of time. On Twitter, people show up for short bursts throughout the day to see what's happening.

The best way to explain Twitter, is that you are shouting down the hallway hoping that somebody hears you. If you're lucky, they might even share what you say or respond to it. People don't typically scroll through your Twitter feed and look back at old content.

On Twitter, it's essential to update your bio and website link. When someone comes across something compelling you say, they know how to learn more about you. Your website link can link back to your business, blog or personal website. You should also include your email address so they can contact you.

Twitter should mostly be used for content that you re-purpose from your other platforms. If you create a video or picture for Instagram or Facebook, you should also post it on Twitter.

You can decide whether you just post the link that goes to your Instagram, or if you copy the caption and post the same post on Twitter. Twitters 280-character limit allows for longer text content than it did when it was first released.

The only other content you should post on Twitter is current events happening around the world. This could be sports, news or trending topics.

For example, if Conor McGregor and Floyd Mayweather are fighting this weekend, you can tweet about it. But if that fight happened two or three years ago, it becomes irrelevant and nobody cares. If it's Super Bowl week, you can tweet about the Super Bowl as much as you want because it's relevant at that time. Unlike the other platforms, people don't really get "content fatigued." You could post ten tweets in a row during the Super Bowl and people will still follow. But if you tweet about the Super Bowl in June, nobody cares.

Twitter is meant for real-time action and real-time updates. If there is a new episode of Billions or a new season of Ozarks, people will be interested. If Americas Got Talent is airing live on Sunday night, you can live-tweet the show all night and use their hashtag. You will likely engage with people that are also watching Americas Got Talent. Just don't expect to get the same engagement if you are tweeting about the show four days later.

So, utilize Twitter in real-time. If you say something funny about something that happened during The Bachelor, and a few people retweet it, you might find your content going viral in The Bachelor community. During those shows, the people watching are very active. So take advantage of that engagement if you are into that particular live event. Search relevant hashtags that align with the show to give yourself a better chance of being discovered.

Beyond current events, you can also use Twitter to stay current or make connections in your niche. Make sure you follow everyone in your industry. Follow experts, news outlets, podcasts, authorities and anyone that might be relevant.

Once you follow them, find ways to engage and interact with them organically. Remember, that doesn't mean you spam them because they likely get plenty of that. It does mean you can respond and engage with thoughtful responses or criticism if that adds value. Whether they respond or not, they will likely see your posts, as will the other people interacting with them, which helps grow your personal brand.

If an authority or celebrity sees your tweet, and it's relevant to their content, they may even retweet you. If you are in the financial services or startup world, and a Venture Capitalist retweets your post, they are amplifying your tweet to everyone that follows them.

Amplification means you are gaining relevant exposure with every one of their followers. Their followers will see your tweet, and over time, your following will grow.

Twitter is especially convenient if you have many niches. For example, the real estate agent that also runs a jewelry business. They could follow everyone in the real estate industry. But they could also the influencers in the jewelry or fashion niche. I'm not saying you should spend all day tweeting at Kylie Jenner, because that's like trying to hit the lottery.

However, I am saying that you should follow the executives, CEO's and business people in your niche. Follow, engage and interact with them as your time allows.

Post news articles, blog posts, events and updates that are relevant to your niche. Again, you also want to retweet content that you find relevant. If one of your favorite fashion influencers sees you supporting their blog, they are far more likely to see your page. If they really like what you have to say, they may retweet you as well.

Facebook

Facebook is the most important social media company in the world. More importantly, it isn't going anywhere anytime soon. Facebook owns many other social media platforms, and it will own more over the course of time.

Facebooks owner, Mark Zuckerberg is too young, too rich, and nobody can afford to acquire their company. Even if they could afford to buy Facebook, he wouldn't sell it so it wouldn't matter.

So, no matter what your opinion is on Facebook, you need to use it for your personal brand. Even if you worry about the politics or privacy of the platform. It's impossible to deny the attention and growth of the platform. It's also impossible to deny its future longevity in the marketplace. Facebook is here to stay.

Here is what your conspiracy aunts and uncles might not tell you. You are in control of what you consume and how you choose to consume it. You can choose to consume politics, drama and news articles, or you can mute or unfollow what you don't like.

Similarly, you can choose to consume content on Facebook if you want. You can also choose to publish content instead. Whatever you choose, I encourage you to take advantage of the huge platform to build your personal brand.

Personally, the drama doesn't bother me. So, I'm able to embrace the platform fully. If the app is no longer serving me, I can close it anytime. Keep in mind that everyone has their own opinion on Facebook as a platform and most include their privacy and political beliefs. Always remember, you are in control of what you consume.

No matter what your beliefs are, that should not preclude you from utilizing a platform that has over two billion users. Facebook will eventually have four billion as the internet continues to expand globally. Don't miss out on that audience because somebody told you Facebook was bad.

On Facebook, you can utilize all forms of content, which makes the platform so unique. You can use your photo and video content of course, but text content is also effective, like on Twitter.

What do I mean by text content?

Meaning, on other platforms, like YouTube, TikTok, and Instagram, you're not going to use text very much besides your caption itself. On Facebook, Twitter and LinkedIn, you will have some posts that are text only.

The goal with your content is to mix up the cadence of your posts to keep your audience engaged. Sometimes you will post photos. Sometimes you will post videos. Occasionally, you will post text, when you want to emphasize the context of your words more than an image.

The goal of your content should be to have a mix between your business, promotional, educational and entertaining posts that keep your audience engaged. If every post is you asking your following to "do something for you" or "support my business," they will become numb to it.

Between your promotional posts, mix in posts about your everyday life.

For example, if you run a fitness brand, post your workouts, meal prep, gym outtakes and promote your brand. Also mix in your hobbies like your pets, children, gardening or whatever you are into. People want to do business with people, not robots. It's your job to tell the full story of your brand.

Engage with your following on a human level, not only a promotional level. If you want to get deep, you can share anything you feel comfortable sharing. However, I personally avoid politics, race and religion.

Why?

It's not that I don't have opinions on those areas of societal culture. But they automatically alienate 50% or more of your following. I'm not saying to not be true to yourself. If you like to post about those things, you can. I just always advise my clients, influencers and friends to not post about those three topics.

Let me give you a quick example: Let's say I was speaking to someone as a Jewish man, and I'm speaking to a Muslim woman. We're never going to speak for half an hour and change each other's minds. She is never going to be converted to say, "You know what? You're right, I'm going to switch to Judaism." She's also never going to convince me to switch to become Muslim.

That example holds true for politics as well. Somebody that likes Donald Trump, arguing with somebody that's a

Democrat is not going to suddenly say, "You know what? You're right, I'm going to switch parties." It just doesn't happen, and so I like to do things that I can win at, and I don't like to do things that have guaranteed failure.

Facebook fan pages & groups

Your personal Facebook is capped at 5,000 people for your friends, family, and acquaintances. The goal of building a personal brand is to create unlimited potential opportunities. Your goal is to connect and reach as many people as possible. Every person could turn into a customer, fan or business relationship. Facebook fan pages allow you to add unlimited amounts of people to your network. So, you will want to create a fan page right away, even if it's small to start. This could be your name if you are developing a personal brand. Your Facebook group could also be your business name or a niche name.

There are car pages on Facebook with millions of members interested in cars. Similarly, there are also millions of people on fan pages for every niche. Whatever your niche is, create a fan page and also join every other relevant group within your niche. Your goal is to become the trusted authority in your niche. Your goal is to have people joining your group to hear more about what you have to say.

How do you get people to join your Facebook group?

If people don't know that you are an expert, they can't follow you. Start by leaving thoughtful and useful advice in the groups you have joined. Don't start spamming the group asking people to join your group, because you will get banned. Instead, start sharing tips that will actually help people. If you help people, they will join your page to learn more.

For example, my friend Ryan Stewman has a Facebook group with over 70,000 salespeople. If you start posting great content and sales tips to help the other people in that group, your name is being seen by tens of thousands of people. The best part, those people are already interested in sales training and it costs you nothing. Keep your content relevant, helpful and informational. Your personal brand will continue to grow.

Once you build somewhat of a following, you will want to start adding Facebook Live into your content strategy. As long as you have at least 500 people in your Facebook group, there's a good chance that your Facebook Lives will get at least a few dozen people. It might not sound like a lot, but it's great practice for public speaking once your personal brand grows large enough to get into public speaking.

You don't just jump on stage and start speaking in front

of 500 people. Start practicing while there are 10 people in the audience, and you will be prepared once that audience grows. Remember, the more you engage with your audience, the more they will engage with you.

Instagram

Instagram is the most emotional platform and acts as a visual calendar for most people throughout their day. Instagram is the first platform people look at in the morning and the last one they check before bed. Some of you are even looking at your Instagram feed between reading pages in this book.

For that reason, most people create their content specifically for Instagram. They then repurpose that content onto every other platform. If you create a photo or video for Instagram, you will also publish that same photo or video to Facebook, Twitter, LinkedIn, etc.

Instagram TV (IGTV) is its own page for any video over 61 seconds. IGTV is where Instagram will showcase your videos to other people that normally don't see your content. On average, only 7% of people see your main feed posts (that number could change in the next hour because the algorithm changes all the time).

You want to mix in IGTV videos sometimes to get more exposure with the people that follow you. The algorithm restricts some of your followers. So, many of those people don't see your typical feed posts. These style videos may also make it onto your YouTube, Twitter, Facebook and LinkedIn because those platforms don't have 60 second time restrictions.

Any video under 60 seconds will show up in your regular feed but could also be published on TikTok. TikTok doesn't allow more than 60-second videos, but that could also change.

On Instagram, you want to mix up your content, just like you do on Facebook. Sometimes post a photo, sometimes a video and utilize your captions to tell the story of that photo or video. Personally, I post more videos than photos because videos create the intrigue of what's next. If a photo tells 1000 words, then a video tells one million. You want to make sure you have videos each week. Those videos should either teach people, show behind the scenes, entertain or make them think.

You are showcasing your life sometimes but bear in mind the reason people engage with your content is for themselves, not for you. This is where most people miss the point of the platform.

Unless you are a Kardashian or aspirational celebrity, people follow you to learn or be entertained. Don't post 16 selfies in a row or 16 videos of you traveling around the world. People can't engage or learn from that; other than how great your life is. If you focus the content on helping them, you will get engagement and build your personal brand.

People often ask, "how often should I post?"

As long as you are posting once per day, if possible, you will have top of mind awareness with your audience. The algorithm will also reward your consistency. You want people to think about you for your personal brand or business, even when you're not there.

Why?

Because mostly, you're not there. So, when they are at lunch with a friend and somebody asks them for a personal trainer or a chef, you want them to think of you and recommend you in those moments. That's why I'm so passionate about social media. Social media creates top of mind awareness that turns into money and opportunity.

On your main feed, it's ok to post more than once per day. But try to post at least once per day if possible. It's ok if you miss a couple of days but try to keep a schedule of 5-7 posts per week.

To make it seem less overwhelming, try to pick a Sunday morning and schedule a few hours. You can film videos and take photographs for the whole month.

If your niche is fashion, beauty, real estate or fitness, make a bunch of short videos, clips and photos that you can save in a file to post throughout the month. Some can be 30 seconds, others 3 minutes and every time length in between.

When you create your content, make sure it stands out, so you don't post another boring workout video. Whether it's backgrounds, colors, props, other people or creative graphics, your goal is to create a pattern interruption.

What is a pattern interruption?

On Instagram, consumers are used to scrolling and consuming. People will scroll for hours and see the same style posts over and over again. They don't stop if every post looks the same. Your goal is to give them a reason to stop scrolling to watch, engage, comment and share your post. Give them a reason to stop by making your post stand out.

You also want to use the Instagram live feature occasionally as well. Similar to the Facebook section, Instagram live is a great way to engage with your audience and home in on your public speaking skills. Instagram live is also a great way to engage with your followers. When you go live, your profile pops up at the top of the story feed so people might see you.

Instagram live also allows you to go live with another person. If that person has a following, you can potentially leverage their audience as well. Even if the lives are only 5 to 20 minutes, they are great additions to the content you are already creating.

Instagram stories have become the most popular section of any social media platform in history. Instagram stories don't need to be perfect. In fact, they encourage quick and on the go daily content sharing that lets your following in on your everyday life. This allows you to take your followers behind the scenes of things that are going on in real-time throughout the day.

This doesn't mean you should post anything and everything. If your followers feel overwhelmed by the number of stories they see, they are more likely to tap through or skip your content altogether.

Make sure to keep things relevant, fun and interesting. Metaphorically speaking, you don't need to post the process of walking up to the house. Instead, show them once you've opened the front door.

Get to the punchline quickly because people are typically using Instagram stories for a quick fix. If they don't find what they are looking for, it's easy for them to skip through your content altogether. A good rule of thumb is don't post more than 20 stories in a 24-hour timespan.

The most recent feature Instagram added was Instagram Reels. Similar to the way Instagram mirrored Snapchats features, they added Instagram Reels to appeal to their TikTok audience. These are short 15-second clips, but will continue to evolve just like every other Instagram feature.

YouTube

YouTube is the best platform for evergreen content. Meaning that anything you post will be relevant for years to come. In most industries, things don't change enough to make a video completely irrelevant. Sure, regulations may change, and new ideas will enter the industry. But the old stuff doesn't really change.

If they do change, there will still be plenty of relevance in your videos. Change also allows you to create new videos to stay current with your audience.

For example, you can make a video about how to tie a tie. You can create a video on how to do a short sale in real estate, how to make a wedding dress or a prom dress. Those things are going to be the same years and years from now, which means your video will always be relevant.

Evergreen content is so important because Google is the number one search engine in the world, and YouTube is the number two search engine. Oh, and Google owns YouTube.

Google owning YouTube makes the platform even more significant. Google favors YouTube content more often than not. If you create a relevant video that gains traction on YouTube, there is a great chance that Google will pull it to the top in their search results. Google trusts YouTube videos because they are far less likely to be faked.

You can fake a news article and there are plenty of digital marketing hacks, but it's much harder to fake a video. For that reason, Google feels comfortable pulling it to the top, which is why it's so important to focus on the titles of your YouTube videos.

When you publish a YouTube video, think about the keywords someone would search for to find your video. Make sure that title is visible everywhere in your content.

YouTubes AI algorithm is so advanced, that it actually does crawl your content.

For example, if you're making a video about a fourplex or flipping a house, you should literally title the video, "Fourplex Flipping House Remodel." By using those literal search terms, people are more likely to find your video when they are searching on Google or YouTube to find content.

Why does that matter?

If you can be ranked on Google or YouTube, you win, and whether you get traffic, eye balls, or authority, it's all worth it. Unlike the other platforms, that traffic doesn't have to happen overnight. You could create a video in your niche that blows up two years later, and you end up gaining unexpected traffic because that video becomes relevant.

The best part about creating YouTube videos?

It costs you nothing and once again, the upside is infinite. You might make your real estate videos one day, but on the weekends, you create karate and pottery tutorials because that's your passion. YouTube allows your creativity to run free and you can create anything you like.

YouTube is meant for longer-form content. You can create videos that are less than 60 seconds. But YouTube was really designed for videos that are 2 minutes to 20+ minutes in length. The production value of your YouTube videos is completely up to you. Some creators have full 4K camera setups, while many others use their iPhone. Some creators take time to edit videos, add music, captions and create a full experience. That's a personal decision based on your brand and the budget you want to spend creating content.

If you shoot a video that will be the highlight of your personal brand for years, you may want to hire someone to produce it for you. If that's not in the budget, check somewhere like Fiverr or Upwork where you may be able to get it done for less. Have them add-in graphics, edit the videos and add captions.

YouTube doesn't have the same pressure to create content that a platform like Instagram has. If you miss a week or a month, then it's not really going to hurt you. YouTube is a place where you can publish videos that live there for years and years. But you do want to have a presence on YouTube no matter what.

You also don't have to treat YouTube like a social media platform. It's not necessary to interact, engage and comment on other videos. Similar to Twitter, YouTube is like shouting down the hallway, waiting to see who hears you. You can publish content and not worry about engaging in comments, or following other people, the way you would on other platforms.

LinkedIn

LinkedIn finally broke through and became cool. How? Because they added photo, video and share-ability. They also added more robust features for search, groups and being able to add people in your industry.

LinkedIn is the only platform where people publicly announce what they do for work. Every person on LinkedIn either has a job, wants a job, owns a company, is looking to hire, open to options or looking to invest.

Everyone on LinkedIn has some sort of financial goal and the platform is filled with people motivated to do business. You're not going to find 13-year old's on LinkedIn there to play and have fun.

Mostly, the platform is filled with 25, 35, up to 65-year old's that have or want careers. That's how you should think about your content on LinkedIn. People probably are not interested in your funny dance video. Instead, publish business-related content.

LinkedIn is where you should post news, thoughts and articles about your industry, hobby or career. You should include videos and photos about your industry each week. Whether you are teaching, edifying yourself, branding your expertise or focusing on engagement. Your activity on LinkedIn should lead to business development.

You also want to add people in your industry each week and continue to grow your network. It's important for you to add or follow influential people in your industry and engage with them. Again, your engagement will create top of mind awareness when a situation comes up.

If you are a business financial consultant looking to land new clients, you should be engaging with CEO's of companies in your industry. At some point during the business cycle, that company will likely be hiring or in need of consulting. You want them to think of you when that time comes.

These are all situations that come up every day on LinkedIn and those jobs are going to people with strong personal brands. It's essential that people know about you when they need your expertise. If they know about you, they can think about you. If they think about you, they can hire you.

Keep your brand image on LinkedIn very clean and to the point. You want to make it very easy for people to see what you do and your credentials for doing it. Don't throw spaghetti at the wall, looking for anything that sticks.

What do I mean by that?

You don't need to place every company you've ever worked with and every project you have ever completed. That information belongs on your website. If they love your profile, they can find the rest of your work on your website. Make it easy to read the highlight reel of the top companies you have worked with and your headline accomplishments. It should be so clean that within 20 seconds of visiting your page, they understand your career.

Once you have everything in place, then you should be continuously posting content. Outside of posting content, your goals should be adding people and interacting on the platform. These are the most useful strategies that will create the most financial upside.

TikTok

Every day I hear people tell me that TikTok is just for kids, which couldn't be further from the truth. Many people assume that it's just a bunch of 14-year old's dancing around. When a platform has hundreds and hundreds of millions of users, and growing, you start to realize the math. There is no way it's just kids. Then when you see legends in the business game like Gary Vaynerchuk and Ed Mylett using the platform, you should also take notice.

When you are building your brand, omnipresence is what matters. If there are hundreds of millions of people paying attention, there is opportunity. With TikTok, there's so much potential to go viral. Even though it may be mostly kids right now, it will eventually expand and age up.

Remember how Facebook first started? When Facebook launched, you couldn't have an account unless you had a .edu address. You physically had to be a college kid to be on Facebook. Now, our grandparents are on Facebook more than we are and our parents post more than we do.

I'm not saying that our grandparents will be dancing on TikTok. But I am saying that the platform will continue to evolve. TikTok has already evolved to include different styles, features and posting abilities.

You want to plant your flag in the ground now and start grabbing your digital real estate, while the platform is so viral. That way, as the platform evolves, you are already there, and you have built a following.

TikTok is the easiest platform to go viral on. Algorithms will always change, but to this point, TikTok is a platform that allows you to catch onto a trending hashtag and gain viral awareness. It might be a trending hashtag, funny topic or a dance that becomes the hot trend across the platform. TikTok will actually show you what those trends are, and you can create content to match those trends. For example, my wife got 1.8 million views on a 10-second video of her reaching her arm out to touch a wall.

On TikTok, you're not utilizing a photo. TikTok is meant for short videos (under 60 seconds) currently. Again, Instagram started off as just a photo platform. Then it added 15-second videos, then 60 seconds and finally IGTV for long-form video. To date, TikTok is for 60 seconds max videos, highlighting 15 seconds or less videos, but that can change over time.

Even if they extend the platform to allow for longer-form content, you will be better off focusing on short content. Focus on creating content 15 seconds or less. Then add in longer content when you really need to explain or teach something further.

TikTok isn't a platform that requires a lot of engagement from you. You don't need to spend time liking, commenting and engaging the way you would on Instagram. You can, but it's not necessary for the algorithm. So far, TikTok has decided that its algorithm is based on content and interaction. The more interaction a video gets, the further it spreads. For that reason, you don't need to spend a lot of time interacting on TikTok because it's just not as necessary to go viral.

The best way to learn TikTok is to watch people who are already successful. That doesn't mean you should just watch people with the biggest followings because dance videos might not be relevant to you.

Instead, find people in your industry or hobby and follow their accounts. See what they are doing successfully and choose what might work for you. Then, create, test and experiment to see what actually does work for you.

Also, make sure to check out the explore page that will show you what's trending and create content quickly to catch those trends. Those trends will likely pass if you wait a week, so time is of the essence on the platform.

You can also build up your TikTok by mentioning and linking your profile on your other platforms. This is cross-platform marketing that works on every platform. If you already have 100,000 followers on Instagram, there's a good chance those people might want to follow you on TikTok as well.

Snapchat

Snapchat is a gorgeous platform. It's fast and ephemeral, but it's mostly being used for text messaging amongst kids internationally. Snapchat has made the platform more difficult to work with than the other social media platforms.

While it certainly has its users, I'm not a huge proponent of it as I am the other platforms. I'm not knocking Snapchat at all. However, their main feature was copied by Instagram stories. Most people create larger followings by utilizing the feature on Instagram, so that's my preferred option.

Snapchat isn't really designed to build, share or create a community like the other platforms. It doesn't have the liking and commenting features either. There also isn't a featured page. I don't want this to sound like I'm ripping Snapchat apart. However, for a personal brand, it's just more difficult to build an audience than the other platforms we have discussed.

You can repurpose your content from Instagram, Twitter, Facebook, TikTok, etc. onto Snapchat. But it doesn't matter much if you like or comment or interact on other people's Snapchats. Their features are much different, and it's utilized far more for text messaging. I'll leave it to you to decide if you want to build a personal brand there. I love what they've done as far as technology. But the usability factor is not conducive for building a personal brand.

Clubhouse

Clubhouse is an audio-based platform where people can learn directly from you like an interactive podcast or live event. People are spending hours consuming content directly from you. Unlike a podcast, the audience can also engage with the host and guest of the podcast or their friends.

The top players on Clubhouse regularly give away free advice, similar to what you would have previously learned in a Mastermind.

Clubhouse allows your audience to understand you on a deeper level. So whether you are speaking to one person or a room with hundreds of people, these listeners are valuable.

Clubhouse is the perfect opportunity for real-time networking in your niche. You can listen to people you admire, or "raise your hand," and they might even bring you on stage to share your thoughts with everyone in the room.

As of now, Clubhouse is an audio-only platform. They don't allow messaging directly, but they do let you link your Instagram and Twitter accounts.

Someone may listen on clubhouse for an hour, but they then want to go follow you because they see your expertise. So they will take it to other platforms to consume your content.

What's great is that you can make a long bio, telling people what you do. Make sure your highlights are at the top of the bio.

They will most likely add DM's and clickable links in the future. But they have already added Instagram clickable links. So make sure to link your profiles!

You will want to go into rooms that are interesting to you or you have expertise in, to consume content and hopefully get pulled onto stage. Your other option is to coordinate with other friends on the platform to host a room.

Whether it's once per week or once per day, it puts you in a position of power because you are hosting the room. Everyone in the audience views you as the authority.

Don't be nervous or shy if there are only 20 people in the audience. Everyone starts somewhere. If you attract the right people and the room is interesting, you give yourself a chance to get lucky! Getting lucky means, if the right person jumps into the room, you may end up with 500 people.

Ultimately, provide value to the people in the room—teach them something, have valuable conversations, and then occasionally include call to actions to buy from you or direct them where you want them to go.

At this point, they have raised money based on a $4 Billion valuation. Clubhouse is attracting a lot of competitors, like Twitter and Facebook, but you can't buy the cool factor that Clubhouse already has.

BitClout

BitClout is the newest social media platform of them all and has a lot of controversy attached to it, which is why it's interesting, exciting, and fascinating. For many years, people have talked about having features that BitClout does.

This is the first time a platform has executed on it and has the money to support it. The platform has many VC investors and hedge fund managers from Sequoia, Andreessen Horowitz, Coinbase Ventures, Winklevoss Capital, Chamath Palihapitiya and Alexis Ohanian. The platform has a powerful backing.

BitClout allows fans/followers and strangers to invest into you, similar to a stock on the stock market.

So let's say your name is John Doe, and your stock is $100. My followers and strangers can invest $20 into you, or $200,000 into you—which would cause your price to fluctuate. Vice versa, you could be investing into other creators you like or look up to!

You don't need to ask people to invest in your profile. Just create good content that's interesting and sharable. BitClout users can make their own decisions about investing in you as a creator.

You will get more engagement if you are engaging with other creators. If you have $10-$20 you can also invest in other creators whether you know them or not.

The content you will create is very similar to Twitter— you can also go back and copy your best tweets/highest engaging photos.

This is a platform that's good for your personal brand. You can also invest in yourself. Whether that's $20 or $200000, that's up to you. You will want to invest something because there is no better investment than betting on yourself.

There are many ways for creators to offer incentives to shareholders, by offering extra content, products, limited releases.

Chapter 9:

Brand Monetization & Other Platforms

If you are looking to monetize your personal brand, there are platforms for creators to do so. You can sell custom products on Etsy. You can create a digital course on platforms like Udemy, Teachable, Coursera and LightSpeed VT.

You can sell memberships to your content on sites like OnlyFans or Patreon. You can also have viewers unlock content on Twitch or YouTube live streams for $1, $5, $10, or more. There are so many ways to make money whether you sell a physical product, entertain people, or teach your subscribers a skill.

Based on the size of your personal brand, you can create your own products and services that fit your niche or passion. This is why I'm so passionate about building a personal brand, because there are so many ways to monetize.

Personally, the way I monetize my personal brand is through top of mind awareness.

For example, let's say someone follows me on Instagram and likes something I have to say about influencer marketing. They know I run a social media marketing agency, but they don't run a business that needs my services.

However, their friend just got an investment to launch a CBD line and needs help telling the world about their brand. That person tells their friend to reach out to my social media agency. That person becomes a customer with our agency, and it all started because I built my personal brand.

That is the power of a personal brand and why it is so important to build your own. If you have a business, your personal brand can turn into business profits, similar to the example I shared above.

Likewise, if you have a passion, you can turn that into a business or side hustle by creating a product or course on one of these platforms.

Even if you never end up selling your own book. Even if you never market your own products, you still want to strongly consider the importance of building your personal brand. It may not sound important to you, but what if your spouse becomes passionate about building their small business?

Or what if you are introduced to a charity in the future that you are passionate about?

It will be a lot easier to help those causes if you have already built a following of people that know and trust you. Your personal brand is important because having a following is useful, not just for you, but also for the people around you and the things you care about.

As you become a recognized expert in your field, brands may start approaching you for consulting deals to speak on your expertise. Consulting and speaking are the highest-paid hourly jobs in the world because there is little to no overhead, besides your time. Brands may also want to sponsor your social media accounts, podcasts and anywhere else you have built an audience.

The important thing to remember, is that opportunities will come up that you can't envision right now. It will require work upfront to build that audience, but it costs you next to nothing and your upside is limitless.

Other Platforms

I don't want to miss any ideas that might inspire you to build your personal brand. There are plenty of other platforms where people build personal brands and businesses. You can sell products on eBay, Etsy or Pinterest. You can become a trusted source for information in communities like Reddit. You can also write articles about your niche and expertise.

If your gift is your ability to write, you should have a blog. There are plenty of blog sites to help you start your writing platform. I would consider wordpress.com or starting a Medium account where people may find your articles and engage with them.

A blog lives with you for years and years, establishing a web presence, along with authority in your niche. Blogs are mainly written posts, adding in photos and videos that tell a story. People visit a blog to learn something compelling or useful for their life.

For example, many people research travel blogs before visiting a new destination. If you are an avid traveler, and have visited 46 states, it's a perfect excuse to start that travel blog. Share your experience, along with some of your favorite pictures and locations from your trip. Someone may read that blog 6 years later on their family trip to Yosemite. Your blog will still be relevant, because Yosemite isn't likely to change much.

Your blog may also become a very valuable traffic source, if your passion for travel turns into a side hustle for a business. What if you have 1000 avid travel fans per month visiting your blog? That's 1000 people that might be interested in your travel retreat business that you start in the future.

Your blog has unlimited potential now and in the future. Your blog will only create more authority as long as you continue to publish insightful and compelling content.

Chapter 10:

Podcasts

Podcasting has become one of the most useful ways to leverage other people's audiences. Podcasting is also a natural way to create content and edify yourself by association.

By appearing on a podcast, you create credibility by interviewing leading authorities in your niche. Likewise, if you can appear on reputable podcasts as a guest, you edify yourself further. It also builds your personal brand because of the niche audience you reach through podcasting.

Podcasting is the only platform that you can't really re-purpose to, only repurpose with. You can't publish your Instagram content to a podcast.

However, you can take the video from a podcast, turn it into 30 second- 1-minute clips for Instagram. Then you can use that same clip on Facebook, LinkedIn and you can post the full episode to YouTube. For many personal brands like

Casey Adams, a podcast becomes the top of their personal brand strategy. He uses his podcast for content on every social platform.

Creating and maintaining your own podcast is a big commitment and not for the faint of heart. To have a successful podcast, you should post at least once per week, preferably twice.

If that doesn't sound sustainable for your schedule, I will give you a little secret. You can schedule a few days and record every episode at once. You could set aside a full weekend, plan your content, and record 16 episodes. It might be draining, but you will have your content booked for 4 months. If you don't have time to record 1-2 per week, this is an option to continue building your personal brand.

Don't start a podcast if you can't commit to one of those options. Most podcasts don't survive past 5 episodes and I don't want that to be you.

Do I want you to make a podcast?

Yes, when you're ready to make that commitment.

Be honest with yourself, because sometimes you're never going to be ready, so you just have to jump into it. If now is not the right time, I'd rather you wait and not do it, instead of starting and quitting.

If you feel like you need the accountability, you can get a co-host to keep the show on track. Make sure that co-host is someone you feel comfortable with and trust. Starting a podcast can become a full-time business. You will have to spend hours preparing and recording with your co-host. Things also get more complicated when you land sponsorships and start generating revenue.

Many people don't start a podcast because they don't think they have anything to say, or enough to talk about. Whether you are considering a solo show or a co-host, keep in mind that you will be interviewing other people. That means less pressure on you and it will help keep the content fresh.

If you are an expert at something, especially in a niche or genre, the audience will want to hear from you as well. Make sure there are enough planned solo episodes, so your audience gets to hear your insights.

I will say podcasts are one of the most ideal things to leveling up your personal brand, but not everybody needs to create a podcast. Since you're reading this book, I am imploring you to go on to other people's podcasts.

I know you have huge aspirations, but I don't expect you to be on Joe Rogan's show right away. I don't think that's necessary either. Getting on small, medium and large podcasts are all useful. Sometimes the small and medium podcasts, will help you get on the large podcasts.

Once you start to climb the ladder, you can leverage those names, showcasing that you are worthy of being interviewed. When you are pitching yourself to appear on other people's podcasts, you are selling yourself. If you can build your personal brand, you are already selling yourself before you open the door. If you have a strong personal brand or following, they are far more likely to say yes.

Building your personal brand makes it clear to other authorities in your niche that you are worth interviewing. They know exactly who you are, what you do, how you can help their audience. If you have your own following, they will view it as an opportunity to reach new listeners for their brand. If those values align, podcasters are likely to say yes.

Remember, they also have the pressure to create new content for their audience. So, they want to say yes if they can.

When reaching out to a podcaster, you are showcasing your bio and how you can serve their audience. Try to keep the initial message to 50 words or less. If they are interested, then you can send them a full email pitch with your bio, social proof and one-page site. Keep it simple and explain why you are a compelling choice for their podcast. Don't be afraid to name drop other shows in their niche that you have appeared on already.

Appearing on other people's podcasts takes minimal effort but must be done at scale. Meaning, your pitch and one-page website won't change. But you might need to send that pitch to 100 podcasts before 6 say yes. I expect you will have better results, but even if only 6-12 say yes over a few months, you are still building your personal brand.

You could pitch yourself or have an assistant/virtual assistant do it for you. You should research and reach out to the podcasts in your niche. The most important key is that you ask and keep asking. It's a simple task, that can be done in your spare time. That means text messages, emails, Instagram DMs, tweets, etc.

When I say that small and medium podcasts are great, I'm not saying that you shouldn't try to appear on large podcasts. I'm saying you should pitch all of them and appear on each one that says yes. This is especially true if you are just starting out. If a podcast only has a few hundred listeners, at least you are practicing telling your brand story and public speaking. That practice will help you when you start appearing on bigger podcasts.

Bigger doesn't necessarily mean better either, especially when it comes to podcasts and building your personal brand. One podcast might have 100,000 listeners for a broad audience, and another could have 6,000 listeners in your niche. The podcast with 6,000 listeners is like drilling for oil and already knowing where the oil is.

Each of those 6,000 listeners have already told you that they are your target audience by subscribing and listening to the podcast. Those listeners are also far more likely to become part of your following once they hear your episode.

Appearing On Podcasts

When you appear on a podcast, keep the self-promotion limited if possible. You will be tempted to tell everyone about your business, service or niche. There will be time to plug your brand during the episode, but that shouldn't be the focus of your interview.

The audience is already listening so your goal is to provide value. Teach them so much that they want to learn more about who you are and what you do. At the end of the episode, you will have a chance to share your social media handles or website URL. If they want to find you after the episode, they can follow you and connect further.

As I mentioned before, the real value of a podcast interview isn't just the audience, but also the content you can create from the interview. If possible, make sure you record the video version of the podcast.

If you are recording live in studio, hire a videographer or ask the host if they feel comfortable sharing the video with you (they almost always will). If you are doing it via Zoom, there is a recording feature that will automatically record the audio and video from the interview.

Once you have the full interview, break those soundbites into clips. These can range from 30 seconds to 3-minute clips that you can use on every other platform. A one-hour podcast interview could end up being 3 to 15 pieces of content. Add this, along with speaking to a new niche audience, and you can see why I'm so bullish on podcasts. The content from a podcast always edifies you, showing other hosts that you are worth interviewing. So, regardless the size of the podcast, it will look good that you are being interviewed.

Make sure that you take the opportunity to promote the host in your clips and posts. Make the content about them as well, not just yourself. If you said yes to appearing on their podcast, you probably already respect them and their platform.

Make sure to promote the episode by creating graphics, clips and content that will edify both you and the host. If you pump up the host, instead of yourself, they will be more likely to re-share the content.

Again, because you're talking about them, they are re-posting about you. So, you ultimately gain more influence for your personal brand. Play chess, not checkers.

Chapter 11:

Building Your Personal Brand Following

Growing a following is the topic I get asked about more than almost anything else in this book. Algorithms change so often, and it can be hard to keep track of the fast-moving world of social media. Facebook and Instagram have become more of a "pay to play" platform. Ultimately, great content always wins. Ads, promotion and shout outs will get people to your personal brand, but only great content will keep them there. You can lead horses to water, but you can't make them drink.

As you gain a following by utilizing the tips laid out in this book, you still have to keep them engaged or they won't stick around for long. Creating great content that serves your niche and has a shareability factor, leads to growing your following long term.

You have heard Gary Vaynerchuk talk about the early days at Wine Library. He was streaming and posting every day, but only getting 12 or 16 viewers on YouTube. Still, he kept posting great content every day.

Eventually, he broke through and grew a large niche personal brand in the wine industry. If you asked Gary, he would say that he was creating "bad content" at the time because streaming was so new. He eventually branched out into other categories and built one of the largest followings in social media history. Authentic great content will always win, even if you switch niches or industries.

Collaborations are key

Collaborations lead to the most targeted follower growth. Why? When you collaborate with someone in your niche, you know their audience is your audience.

For example, if you are a fitness influencer that loves basketball, you could reach out to other influencers that already have a following. Your goal is to see if they want to create content together that will serve both of your personal brands.

If you created entertaining videos with somebody like @dribble2much, the videos would go viral on his account.

When his followers see you featured in his video, they are more likely to follow you as well because you're posting basketball content with him.

That same idea applies to your at-home cooking channel. It's great to create organic content every day. But you have a better chance to grow your niche following, if you teamed up with other chefs in your neighborhood. If four people all have a similar following, consider doing a live stream together on Sunday nights at 6 o clock. Now, you are all getting similar exposure to other niche followings, and everybody wins.

These collaborations don't happen on their own, and if it were easy, everyone would do them. Remember the high school prom theory. When everyone is at prom to dance, but nobody wants to be the one to get rejected after asking someone else to dance. So, everyone stands on the sideline and nobody ever dances. This is the same situation. Sometimes you have to be the one to ask other creators to dance. Creators want to dance as well, whether they play basketball, or have a cooking show. It's your job to be the brave one and ask them to dance.

Shout-out Pages

In every niche, there are shout out pages that have built large followings. Those pages are always looking for more content, and you can pay them for promotion.

For example, if you are a travel influencer that creates stunning travel videos. There are thousands of travel pages looking for engaging content. They make thousands of posts every year, so they need your content. They also have built their audience around the niche you are trying to reach. So, anyone that follows you from those shout out pages, is likely interested in your personal brand.

If the post is self-promoting, or you want them to tag you, they may charge you a small fee to post your content. By small fee, I mean $20-$50. Even the huge pages only charge a few hundred dollars to post to their millions of niche followers. Shout outs can get expensive if you start posting on those huge pages. So, I would rather you spend $0-$50 for a post that is very specific to your niche audience.

Providing Value

If you are publishing content that is educational, interesting or entertaining, people are more likely to share it. So many people miss the point of sharing content. Their content is vain and only serves them, instead of their audience.

If you can teach or entertain someone, they are more likely to tag their friends and re-share your content. This is the best way to organically grow your following. People that already follow you, and share your content, are recommending you to their followers. It's free and effective, just make sure the content is valuable and not self-promotional.

Another way to grow your social media following is to follow people that are already authorities in your niche. Once you follow them, start engaging and commenting on their posts. Their followers will see it and you may gain a consistent following. That is, as long as you are being an insightful voice in the comments. If they share a post on "3 tips to building your personal brand," that is your chance to add other tips that helped you.

If you have the ambition to grow a large personal brand, try setting alerts on your favorite niche influencers posts. When you see them post, leave insightful comments that add value to that post. If people see your witty or insightful comment, they are more inclined to check out your page. If the content on your page is great, they are more likely to follow you.

Chapter 12:

Getting Featured & Pitchng Yourself

Sliding into DM's has become a popular term, typically related to dating. Sliding into DM's is also the best way to engage with people on social media. Sliding into the DM's means talking to people. Your goal is to engage and message people with large audiences to keep yourself on their radar.

If they like what you have to say, you can send them content to feature on their own niche page. At this point, you can ask them to post your content and they will either do it for free, or they may charge you a small fee. Similar to your podcast outreach, the more pages you message, the better your results will be.

You can also build your personal brand by being featured in the press, news, blogs or other people's podcasts.

These are other mediums that will create credibility and introduce you to new audiences.

When someone Googles your name, these are the types of content that get featured first. The goal of your pitch is to be interesting, share your story and provide value to their platform. Again, this strategy doesn't usually cost money. It does require a lot of effort to be the talking head of your brand.

These strategies work well for growing your business. But don't forget about your hobbies and passions. For example, you might be in the car industry, but you love playing poker. You just won a Las Vegas poker tournament and a poker outlet wants to interview you for the article. Just because the article is about poker, doesn't mean that poker players couldn't also be interested in cars. Somebody could see the article, click the link back to your website. They saw you in a poker article, but eventually buy a car from you. There are so many missed opportunities because people limit their exposure to only one niche.

Pitching Yourself

For every marketer that yells how great they are, there are hundreds more that don't know how to pitch themselves. I want you to think about something for a second. Podcasts average one to three episodes per week. That means a podcaster averages between 52 and 156 episodes per year. I don't know about you, but I don't know 156 people that I want to ask to be on my podcast each year. Then year two, three and four, the numbers really start to add up. The motivated podcaster will need thousands of guests in the shows lifetime, so they need you.

The same goes for getting press, guest blog posts, magazine articles or newspaper features. Every writer in the world has the pressure to create and write new compelling stories. After they finish one, they need more and that's where you come in. Your job is to tell your story and make it easier for them to tell it for you.

I often say that a closed mouth doesn't get fed. If you simply ask over and over, you will eventually get a yes. Once one outlet says yes, now you can leverage that yes when you pitch the next outlet. Each yes creates a snowball effect and it gets easier to pitch your story.

Your goal is to ask as many relevant podcasts, bloggers, press outlets and podcasts as possible. Use that media and those appearances to land bigger outlets. People will see you as press and feature worthy once they see that others have already told your story.

Your email or DM headline should be your top headline that will get their attention. The headline is where they will decide if they open or read the rest of your pitch. After the headline, you want to include your story pitch and also your ask. If they have a podcast or write for a news outlet, they may already know why you are reaching out, but be sure to be specific.

"I would love to be featured on your show. I would love to be interviewed on your podcast because (pitch)." Then craft your compelling pitch, keeping in mind how you can serve their audience.

What makes you a great guest? Once you get them to read your headline, your pitch and story will ultimately decide if they say yes. If they say yes, that's when your one-page website or PDF comes into play.

You already created your one-page website. You should also turn that into a shareable PDF one-pager for offline easy access sharing. This is another asset that tells your full story after they show interest in interviewing you.

Make sure to include a photo, your resume, social proof and any story that will resonate with people. If you were in the Guinness Book Of World Records, mention it. If you were the youngest real estate agent to sell the most real estate at Coldwell Banker, include that. If your beauty blog has over

2 million views, lead with that too. This is where you must be bold and very direct about your accomplishments. Break them down into sentences, not paragraphs.

Once you've built your social media following, you want to start promoting those accomplishments on your one-page PDF. Once you hit 10,000 followers, or a significant milestone, make sure they know that. Your audience makes you a more compelling guest and as you keep growing your brand, these outlets will start reaching out to you.

If you have 100,000 followers on Instagram, and another 50,000 on Facebook, people will be more interested in interviewing you. Now, they view your brand as an asset and opportunity to build their following. So, make sure to include any substantial followings on your one-pager and update that as your personal brand grows.

You will also want to include an email for them to contact you. Add your email in case they don't see the message right away or hang onto your PDF for future considerations. They may not want to interview you now but may revisit your story if your niche becomes more relevant in the news. You can also include a phone number if you have a business number that you don't mind sharing.

On your PDF, make sure your designer adds a clickable link to your Linktree site as well. Make it easy for them to find your social media pages and your relevant links.

Finally, in your pitch, include a short sign off with a call to action that highlights your ask again. "I look forward to speaking with you about being a guest on your podcast." Your signature at the bottom should include your name, title, phone number and a link back to your personal brand.

Chapter 13:

Starting Your Journey: Omnipresence

Kevin Hart, The Rock, Mark Cuban and Elon Musk. These are a few of the people that consistently post content and understand the importance of building an omnipresent brand. Every one of them has built more wealth than they could ever spend in multiple lifetimes.

So why do they do it?

They understand the importance of omnipresence and top of mind awareness.

When an A-list comedy script is greenlit, Kevin Hart wants to be the first person they call.

When a multi-million-dollar sports league needs a facelift and re-launch, The Rock wants to be the first person they think about.

When an emerging tech unicorn is looking for guidance or funding, Mark Cuban wants that first meeting.

Elon Musk is busy changing the world, but he also realizes the importance of his personal brand. Imagine if Elon Musk didn't share his vision or speak to his audience. It would be up to consumers and media to try to draw their own conclusions about what he is doing. Elon wants to be the voice of his visions and he does that by having an omnipresent personal brand.

Before any of these people were global icons, they were simply Kevin, Dwayne, Mark and Elon. They were people just like you with big ambitions, ideas and a work ethic. None of this happens overnight, and you have to start somewhere.

Kevin Hart was once a shoe salesman who decided he was going to be a comedian. He pounded the pavement under the stage name Lil' Kev The Bastard. He spent years performing at small comedy clubs before he ever tasted success.

The Rock was a football player and began his wrestling career in the USWA under the stage name Flex Kavanah before being noticed by the WWE.

Mark Cuban owned a bar, gave disco lessons and started a chain letter in college before he ever started Micro Solutions.

Elon Musk is an anomaly, who sold his first software at age 12. But even Elon Musk has reinvented himself and his companies over and over again throughout his career.

The reason I am sharing these examples is to give you permission to start from wherever you are. More importantly, I am giving you permission to define yourself. Tell the world who you are and what you do. This is your opportunity to reinvent yourself and document your journey from step 1. You can be anyone you want to be, as long as you have the courage to tell your story.

2 years ago, if I told you that I would start a retail sports card shop in the middle of a pandemic, where most businesses were downsizing or moving fully online, you might have called me crazy. You still might. But sports cards were always a passion of mine, so when the sports card industry got hot, I decided to start documenting what I was doing.

Every day on my social media pages, I would post new cards I was buying and share exactly what I was doing. I didn't tell the world that I was starting a card shop, but I was documenting my journey. Eventually, that passion led me to launch Cards & Coffee. When you follow your passion and document the process, the opportunities will find you.

Once you build your personal resume of what you do, you might want to consider reaching out to an expert in your industry. Depending on what you have to offer, they may be willing to pay you or provide opportunities that will set you up for future success.

One mistake that most people make, is reaching out to an expert asking, "how can I provide value?" That question shows that you haven't done your homework. These are busy and already successful people. They are getting hundreds of messages every week from people looking for opportunities.

Prepare first and understand exactly how your skills will help them accomplish their goals. Maybe you are a video producer. Maybe you create graphics, or maybe you are the best salesperson and can offer to sell their products or services.

It only takes one opportunity to change your life forever. By documenting your journey, being consistent and building an omnipresent personal brand, you set yourself up for "once in a lifetime" opportunities.

If you are just getting started, you might not be able to relate with Kevin Hart or The Rock. But real people change their lives every day because they decided to build their personal brand and were bold enough to ask for an opportunity.

One day I was checking my Instagram DM's and saw an account @dribble2much. He had been messaging me with videos of him dribbling and teaching kids how to get better at basketball. He didn't ask for anything, instead he shared his idea of doing a basketball camp in LA. He didn't have any money but had the skills and was determined to get an opportunity. At first, I thought what he was doing was pretty cool, but I didn't know if he was committed.

He continued to ask, so I decided to give him a shot to come out for 4 days and work with me. I flew him out to LA and 4 days, turned into 4 months because I saw how hard he worked. During that 4 months, I let him stay with me under one condition: Every day he had to DM celebrities and athletes, offering to train their kids for free.

One Friday, he had the opportunity to train Diddy's son. Of course, I told him I would drive him.

We went to Diddy's house and while he was training Diddy's son, I filmed a few videos of them playing basketball. Diddy's son posted the video and it got some traction, but the real win happened a few days later. In the middle of the night he knocked on my door freaking out because his Instagram notifications were going crazy. There was so much engagement that we couldn't figure out where it was coming from. It looked like his phone was melting.

Sure enough, Diddy had reposted the video of @dribble2much training his son. That was his once in a lifetime opportunity and his life changed forever. Athletes and celebrities started reaching out, asking him to train them.

That video landed him opportunities to train stars like Steph Curry, Kevin Durant, Russell Westbrook, Drake, 2Chainz and many others. He was sleeping on my couch one day, and almost overnight becomes one of the most sought-after basketball trainers in the world.

In 2019, he had another once in a lifetime opportunity. We were at a bowling alley and I could see him freaking out again. I immediately had flashbacks. It was a video that Drake posted of them playing basketball.

The caption was simply "Happy Birthday @Dribble2much." The rest is history. @Dribble2much now has over 1.4 million followers. Today he trains the highest-level athletes and celebrities in the world, all because he was willing to bet on himself.

His big break may have happened overnight, but he had spent years working on his skills, training people, posting content and building his personal brand. There is no such thing as an overnight success, but by building your personal brand, you are setting yourself up to be noticed. It only takes one opportunity to change your life forever.

What were his startup costs? A basketball and his time. If you are hungry for change and are willing to invest the time, you are setting yourself up for future opportunities that will change your life forever.

Stories like @Dribble2much happen more often than you think.

Kevin Ostaj is one of the most well-known photographers & videographers in the world. At one point in his life, he was flying from Chicago to LA every week. He was broke and sleeping in a closet at 1600 Vine St. He knew he had the talent and had built his personal brand that showed his skills. He just needed the exposure. 1600 Vine St was where a lot of the influencers lived and the inspiration for the app "Vine."

Kevin worked for free in exchange for shoutouts and exposure from these influencers. Even though he wasn't being paid, he was showcasing his work to the world and eventually people noticed. By people I mean me. I loved his work and offered him a paid position to work with me at my social media agency.

His brand continued to grow, and people were starting to notice his work. One day my wedding planner reached out to me and asked if I had a great videographer for an event she was working on. Because Kevin had been doing great work for me, my top of mind awareness made me think of him right away.

I made the introduction and Kevin landed the opportunity to film content for her upcoming celebrity event. That event happened to be a Kardashian event, and became Kevin's "once in a lifetime opportunity." At the event, he met Paris Hilton and she offered him a position to film for her.

Now, I rarely see my videographer because he's flying all over the world filming for Paris Hilton. He's filmed major events, festivals, projects with Drake, Martin Garrix and countless celebrities. All of it started because he built his personal brand and set himself up for future success.

Made in United States
North Haven, CT
07 October 2021

10192318R00070